FOREWORD

Many people beli[...]et another soulless inner ur[...] concrete and the traffic li[...]g to be unearthed. Howev[...]story that you read about i[...]r even traditional 'local' [...]Shepherds Bush is hardly remarkable for the number of important people who have lived there or for its wealth of architectural merit. Yet the fascination of studying the local history of a place like Shepherds Bush is precisely because it is so typical: such a microcosm of the rapid urban development that took place particularly in the last quarter of the 19th century. By finding out about our own local history we learn about the cultural, social, economic and political forces that have moulded the landscape not only of Shepherds Bush, but of London as a whole.

Shepherds Bush up to now has not been well served by local histories or local historians; that is why I welcome this pioneering volume by that redoubtable band of local people in the Shepherds Bush Local History Society who have now put the area firmly on the local history map. Since it was founded in 1980 the Society has been assiduous in researching the history of the area, particularly over the last hundred years, and has produced two well-received oral histories: 'Bill Massey - Trade Unionist' and 'George Mason - Councillor'. The study of our local history unites all generations and cultures and explains the dynamic and ever-changing processes whereby modern day Shepherds Bush became a varied mix of cultures and classes. It encourages cross-generational contact through the use of oral history and reminiscence, and can help to provide a sense of identity for many people living in the area.

In an era when the traditions, heritage, and culture of ordinary people often seem to be submerged by the antiseptic and superficial form of 'popular culture', as depicted by television and the tabloid press, it is welcoming and re-assuring to come across local historians who firmly believe that the history of ordinary people in an inner London suburb is worthy of study for its own sake.

So if you are interested in researching any aspect of your local history or helping others to do the same, search out all your old photographs, postcards, newspaper cuttings and bring them and yourself to the Shepherds Bush Local History Society. Remember, you could be helping to compile the successor to this very impressive first edition of the local history of Shepherds Bush.

Ivan Gibbons

Sheep in Shepherds Bush Road passing over the L&SW railway, 1905

SHEPHERDS BUSH GREEN - AN INTRODUCTION

Shepherds Bush Green is a triangular open space of eight acres situated in West London at the junction of Uxbridge Road, Goldhawk Road and Holland Park Avenue. Up until about one hundred years ago it was simply a village green surrounded by a few cottages, farmland and nurseries. It is a very old municipal open space and why it became known as Shepherds Bush is a mystery, but it is a known fact that a man called Sheppard centuries ago owned some land in the area.

Another possibility is, that being a drove road from the West on the way to London, this was a convenient place for shepherds to rest their flocks before the final few miles into the market at Smithfield. One explanation which is much more romantic than the others is that, according to a clergyman, who sent a letter to the Daily Telegraph and signed himself 'A Hedgerow Parson', a shepherd's bush was an ancient white thorn the shape of an inverted mushroom. The upper part of the bush would be smooth and forming a shallow cup where the shepherd would lie resting while watching his flock graze...

So lonely and dark was the place, and so infested with rough characters, that an old lady at the turn of the century remembers that when she was a child her father took care to be equipped with a lantern and pistol when called to escort his family to a neighbour's house. The story also went, according to the old lady, that a shepherd had been murdered while resting on the green and his body thrown into the bushes.

Very little has been recorded about Shepherds Bush before the 18th century but one story which survives relates to a building which stood on the corner of Goldhawk Road and the Green (now the Bush Hotel). This building was a much-frequented inn which was hired by Miles Syndercombe for the purpose of assassinating Oliver Cromwell on his way to Hampton Court in January 1657. The house was owned by a Henry Busby, who was coachman to the Earl of Salisbury. The road at this point was so narrow and bad that carriages were forced to go slowly. Syndercombe had invented a machine-gun which was to be loaded with twelve bullets and discharged at Cromwell's coach as he passed by. If the plot had been successful, the coach with Cromwell and other passengers would have been completely destroyed but Syndercombe was betrayed by one of his accomplices. When tried, Syndercombe denied the plot but he was found guilty and the sentence of the court was that he 'be put from hence to the prison of the Tower of London, from whence he came, and thence be drawn upon a hurdle through the streets of London to Tyburn there to be hanged on a gallows until he be half dead, and then cut down, and his entrails and bowels taken out and burnt in his face or sight, and his body divided into four quarters, and be disposed of as his Highness shall think fit'. As it was expected that an attempt would be made to rescue Syndercombe, the Protector gave particular orders to guard him well in the Tower, but when the keepers went to call him in the morning he was found dead in his bed. Cromwell was very disturbed at this for instead of getting a useful confession out of this man he found himself accused of causing him to be poisoned.

The original inn hired by Syndercombe was pulled down about 1770 and a small one story thatched cottage was built on the spot. It was at one time occupied by a Mr. Galloway who was an eminent engineer.

AREA AROUND SHEPHERDS BUSH GREEN 1741

Surveyed by John Rocque

Shepherds Bush was on the North High Way - now the Uxbridge Road. It was a triangular green at this stage with the other two sides of the triangle leading to Brook Green Lane - now Shepherds Bush Road and Gold Lock Lane - now Goldhawk Road.

A gibbet had been built on the eastern apex of the Green and there were few buildings around the Green. Most were along the north side i.e. the North High Way, the main building to the north of the Green being an inn - today the Wellington Inn (although it slightly

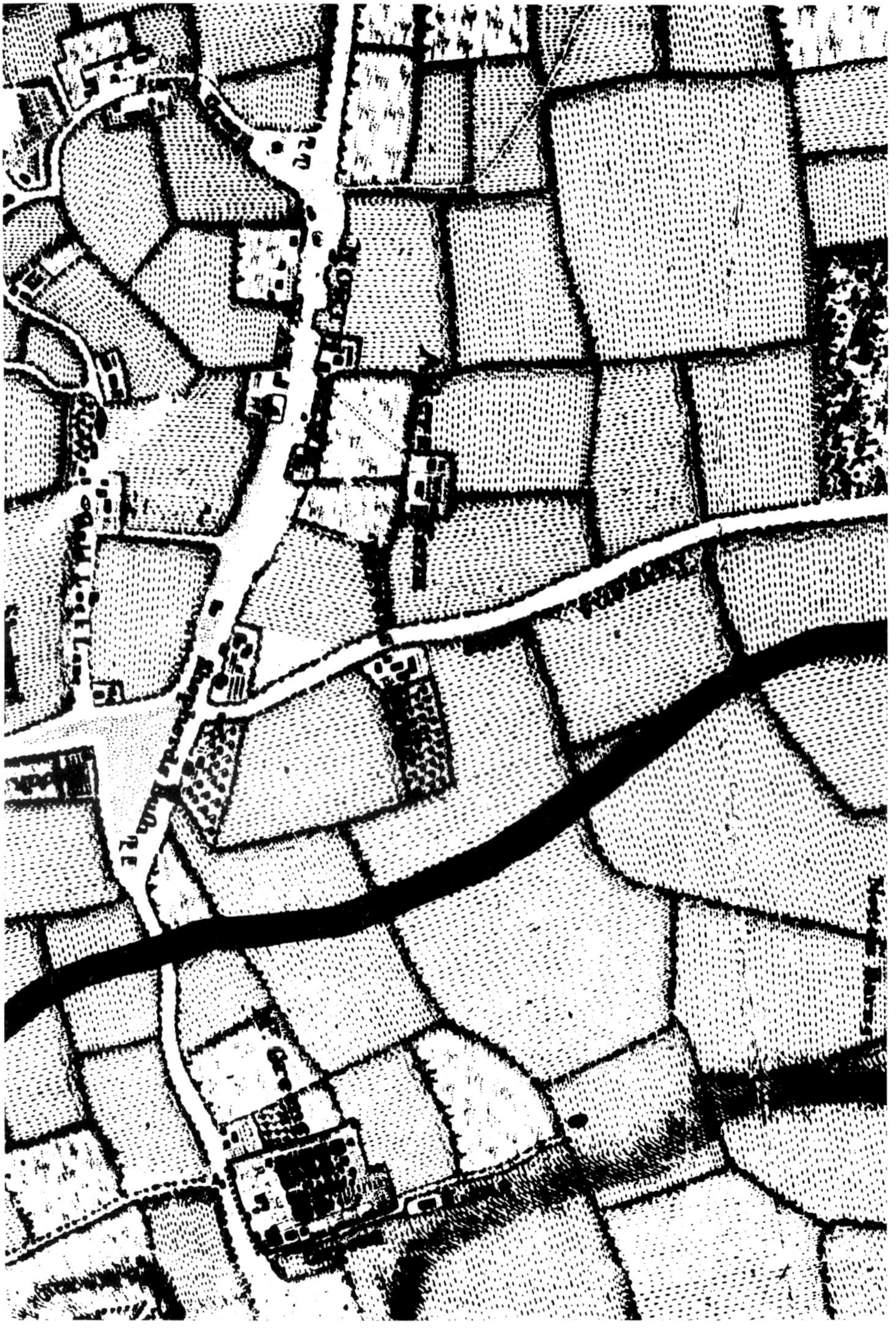

John Rocque, 1741

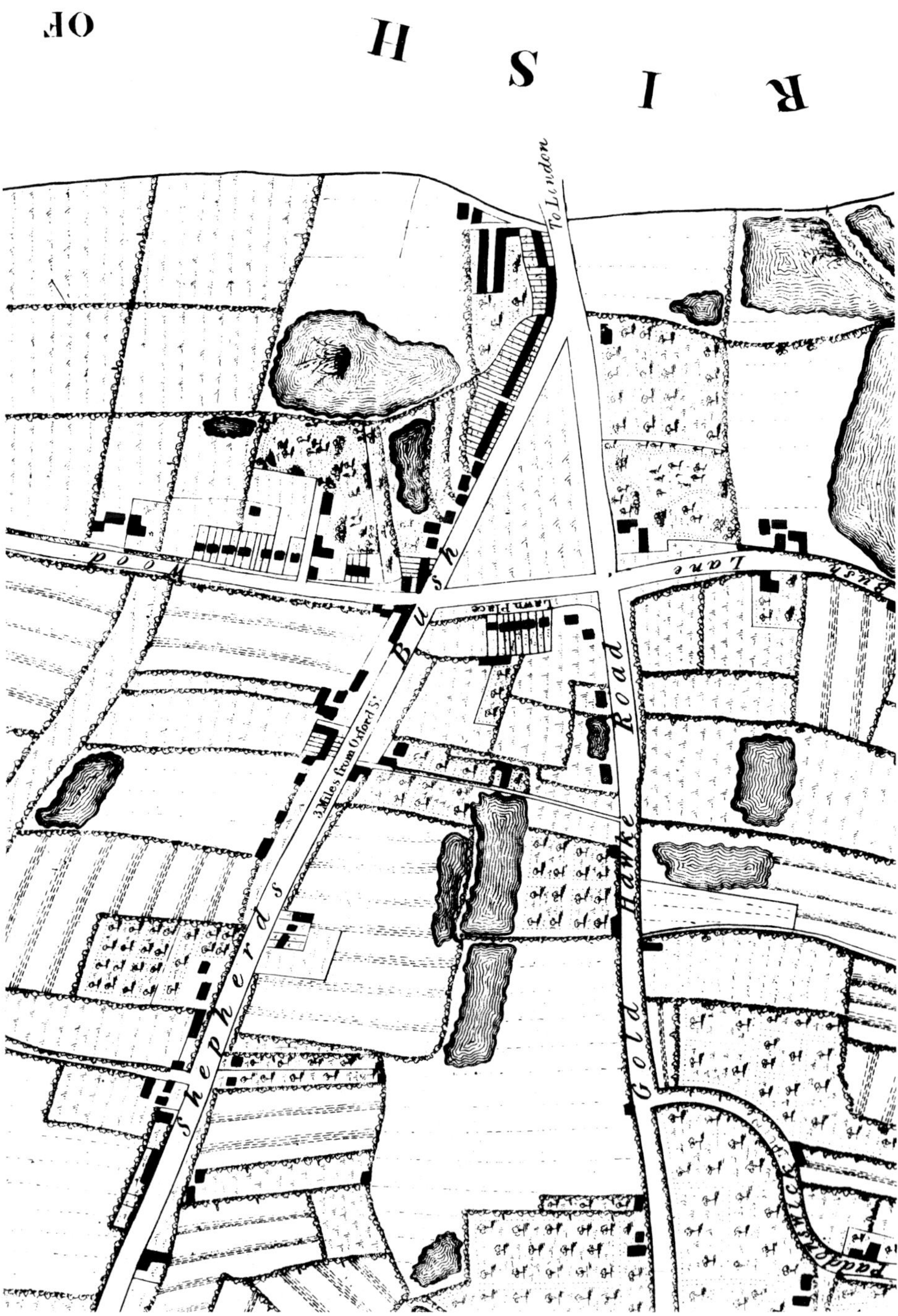

John Slater, 1830

changed position due to rebuilding just after the turn of the century). The building at the corner of the west side of the Green and Gold Lock Lane was the Syndercombe Cottage later the site of the White Horse Brewery and today the Bush Hotel. There was also a building at the corner of the south side of the Green and Brook Green Lane, probably a dwelling house.

The land around the Green was laid out in fields separated by hedgerows with a wooded area to the north of the Green around the inn. This area was in the countryside beyond a much smaller London. Transport was difficult, either walking or by horse or carriage or coach but many could not afford to pay for transport, and so lived very close to their work in London which was very overcrowded at this stage. The land around the Green was owned or leased by farmers who supplied the city with dairy produce and fresh vegetables daily as well as growing grain and producing meat.

AREA AROUND SHEPHERDS BUSH GREEN 1830

Surveyed by John Slater

Parish of Hammersmith - population 1821 - 8,000
1830 - 12,500

This shows a definite change in the landscape of the area since 1741. It was no longer a totally rural area - ribbon development had occured along the main roads leading to London reflecting advances in transport. Roads were much better and there were better services into and out of London which had become so overcrowded that many people did not want to live in the noise and pollution of the city any longer.

The northern part of the Green was now occupied by new rows of terraces as well as some of the older buildings, e.g. the inn. The area behind these buildings is now shown as flooded - possibly due to the removal of clay for brick making - something which affected many parts of the suburbs.

A row of semidetached houses was also built along the west side of the Green which was given the name

Lawn Place. There was little building development on the south side of the Green.

The road names had also changed at this stage. The North High Way is now referred to as Shepherds Bush, the Gold Lock Lane becomes the Gold Hawke Road and the part of Brook Green Lane nearest Shepherds Bush becomes Shepherds Bush Lane.

AREA AROUND SHEPHERDS BUSH GREEN 1853

This map is a tithe map in which the number on each property links it to an entry in a book which gives details of the land owners, tenants, size and value.

At this time two sides of the Green have been built up. The south side is still largely open land. The house at the corner of Shepherds Bush Road was known as the Grange. It was occupied with its stables, garden and paddocks by a Mr. Smith. Some of the land was part of the Charecroft Estate owned by the Camden Charity. The land to the east of Mr. Smith's, also part of the Charecroft Estate, was let to William Plimley who was there until 1864. The area was used partly as a nursery and partly as a market garden. Mr. Plimley had fine pineapples grown in his 'forcing pinery'.

The plot of land to the east of this had been sold or leased for housing development, i.e. Richmond Road - now Richmond Way.

The west side of the Green is divided into even more plots beside those of Lawn Place. The building at the corner of New Road - now Goldhawk Road - is the White Horse Brewery which is now the Bush Hotel.

The north side of the Green is almost totally built up with the building of new terraced houses extending along Providence Place - now Shepherds Bush Place. Further expansion in this direction was blocked by the land owned by the Railway, and that attached to Wood House to the east of Wood Lane. There is a pond between these lands and the area around it is owned and worked as a market garden by George Bridge who has let his land fronting on the road for housing and gardens. Some of this land was owned by the Latymer

Tithe Map, 1853

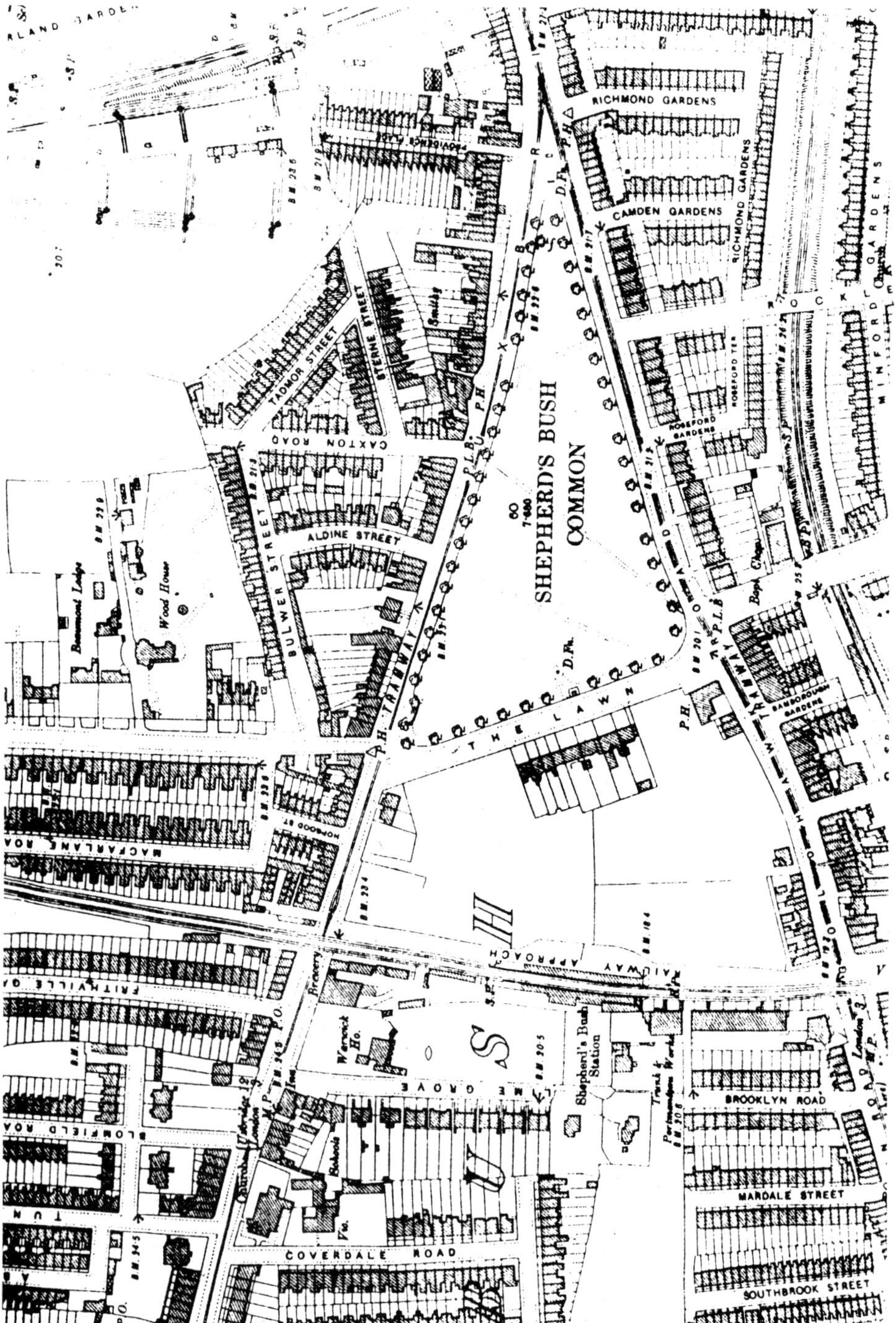

Ordnance Survey 1896

Charity. The public house - later the Wellington - was occupied by James Higgs.

Transport had become much better generally at this stage with the spread of the railways. Although the railway passed through the area - on the east of the map - it did not yet have a station for passengers and so the very fast development which occured with the use of rail transportation was just about to start - a paradise for land speculation.

AREA AROUND SHEPHERDS BUSH GREEN 1896

Within the forty years since the 1853 map the character of this area has changed dramatically. The Green has been planted with trees around the edges and a drinking fountain installed at the west end. It has become built up on all sides although less to the west than elsewhere and the area now has an urban rather than rural character. The market gardens have largely been replaced by rows and rows of terraced houses built speculatively for occupation by the lower middle class white collar workers who worked in the city. There were now three railway stations in the area. The Shepherds Bush station on the Metropolitan railway - now the market office at Shepherds Bush market - the Uxbridge Road station to the east of the Green on the corner of Norland Road - now the site of the Shepherds Bush roundabout - and the Shepherds Bush station on the L. & SWR Kensington and Richmond Line at Shepherds Bush Road. There are also horsetrams running into central London and along the Uxbridge and Goldhawk Roads.

The character of many of the buildings around the Green also changed since 1853. The buildings on the north side of the Green along the Uxbridge Road whereas in 1853 they were dwelling houses, now they provided the many services needed by the people who lived in the surrounding streets. The Green was a focus of life for the area.

Some of the services provided along the north side of the Green at this stage were: firewood merchants, builders, water softener and sterilization company, coal merchants, building society (even then), Home & Colonial grocery store, bootmaker, ironmonger, dyer, tobacconist, Lockharts Cocoa Rooms (before Lyons Tea Rooms), photographer, musical instrument dealer, ham & beef dealer, tailor, newsagent, butcher, fruiterer & florist, wheelwright, furniture dealer, hairdressser, fried fish shop, dressmaker, undertaker, plumber, naturalist (taxidermist), coachbuilder, saddler, zinc worker, oil man (hardware shop), the Wellington Cycle shop, printer, draper, pawnbroker, estate agent as well as three public houses, The Mail Coach, The Wellington and The Beaumont Arms.

From the above list you can see how good a commercial centre the Green was, and this was only the north side. There were also shops along the eastern part of the south side with watchmakers & jewellers, tarpaulin manufacturers, chemist, fishmonger, baker, dairyman as well as other types of shops already mentioned on the north side.

The Lawn and most of the south side of the Green remained as mainly residential property although there were some professionals living and working there, solicitors, surgeons, dentists, a professor of music and a Ladies School at 58 The Lawn run by Mrs & Miss Saunders.

There are still some large old residences behind the new development north of the Green, Wood House and Beaumont Lodge. The grounds of Wood House were used for a balloon exhibition in 1894.

Shepherds Bush Green was at this time the busy centre of a growing and prospering suburb of London.

Uxbridge Road, 1893

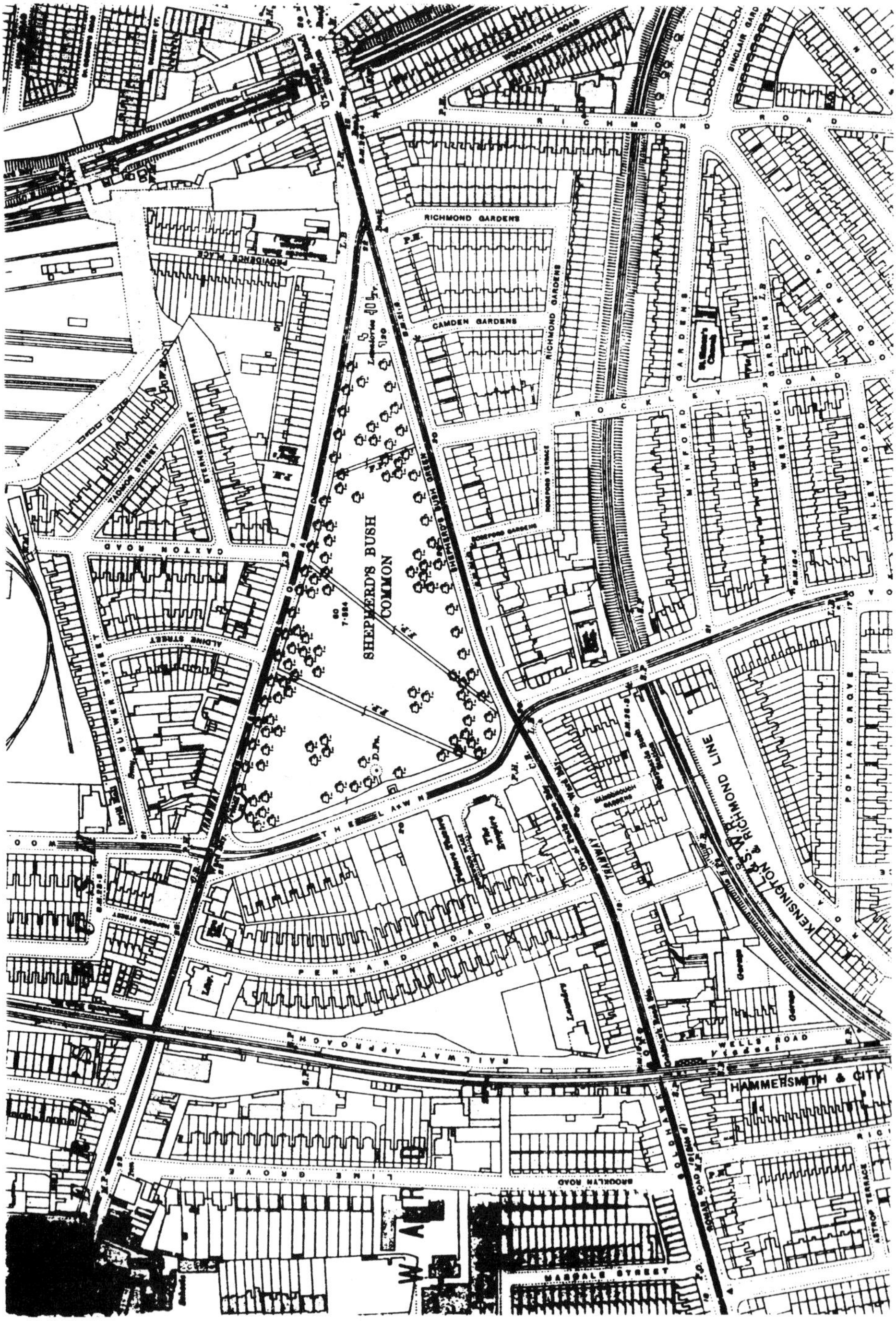

Ordnance Survey 1916

AREA AROUND SHEPHERDS BUSH GREEN c. 1916

This period sees the whole of the area around the Green built up. Pennard Road has been built on the last open area to the west of the Green. Wood House and Beaumont Lodge have been demolished and the land taken over by the railways as a depot. There has also been a lot of rebuilding. On the west side of the Green the original houses of The Lawn have been demolished and a new row of houses has been built as well as a Picture Theatre or cinema and The Empire, a variety theatre. The public house (the Bush Hotel) on the corner of the Goldhawk Road has been rebuilt. The buildings along the Uxbridge Road on the north side of the Green have also been demolished and rebuilt as a stately terrace instead of a mixture of various styles and dates.

There have also been some changes in the railway situation. Shepherds Bush station on the Metropolitan Line has been closed and replaced by two new stations on the main roads, i.e. Goldhawk Road station and a new Shepherds Bush (Met.) station on the Uxbridge Road. A new electric railway - the Central Line - had reached Shepherds Bush in 1900 and this station is at the eastern apex of the Green near the older Uxbridge Road station. This new station served what was now Shepherds Bush's most famous attraction, the White City exhibition centre whose entrance was beside the station. This entrance led to a series of very large elevated halls which stretched all the way to Wood Lane. These halls contained various trade exhibits and through there thousands of people walked to reach the main exhibition site on the other side of Wood Lane. The main site is now occupied by the BBC Television Centre, Hammersmith Park and the White City Estate. Some of the halls remain today and are used for indoor sports.

The Uxbridge Road side of the Green remains the main commercial and retail section with many of the earlier businesses remaining, some now located in better premises, due to rebuilding. New businesses in the area included a Lyon's Tea Shop near the tube station and the exhibition entrance, to compete with Lockharts Cocoa

Rooms. W.H. Smith has opened a book shop in the same area and Marks & Spencer has also opened a store here.

Entertainment became more important and a number of establishments with names like Bazaar Funland, Automatic Bazaar and Victoria Bazaar appeared as well as two theatres on the west side. Slightly further away a film studio was established in Lime Grove in 1910 - now the BBC Studios.

The character of the south side of the Green remained unchanged - mainly private houses between Shepherds Bush Road and Camden Gardens with commercial premises further east.

AREA AROUND SHEPHERDS BUSH GREEN c. 1930

Already at this stage there are signs that the era of expansion and prosperity has gone. Although two new cinemas have been built, the Pavilion on the west side of the Green in 1923 and the Silver Cinema opposite the Shepherds Bush Metropolitan station on the Uxbridge Road, there are signs of a rundown in other services, for example the railway line to the south on the Shepherds Bush Road is now closed.

There are a few changes in the businesses along the Uxbridge Road side of the Green, the Victoria Bazaar has been replaced by a grocer's shop and then an amusement arcade. The Automatic Bazaar has been replaced by the Star Cinema which was a very small establishment near the Beaumont public house. New enterprises have appeared described as 'motor accessories' and 'car manufacturers' (probably a garage). Woolworth store opened about this time beside the Wellington public house.

The White City exhibition centre is still being used for exhibitions and the stadium for greyhound racing and athletic meetings.

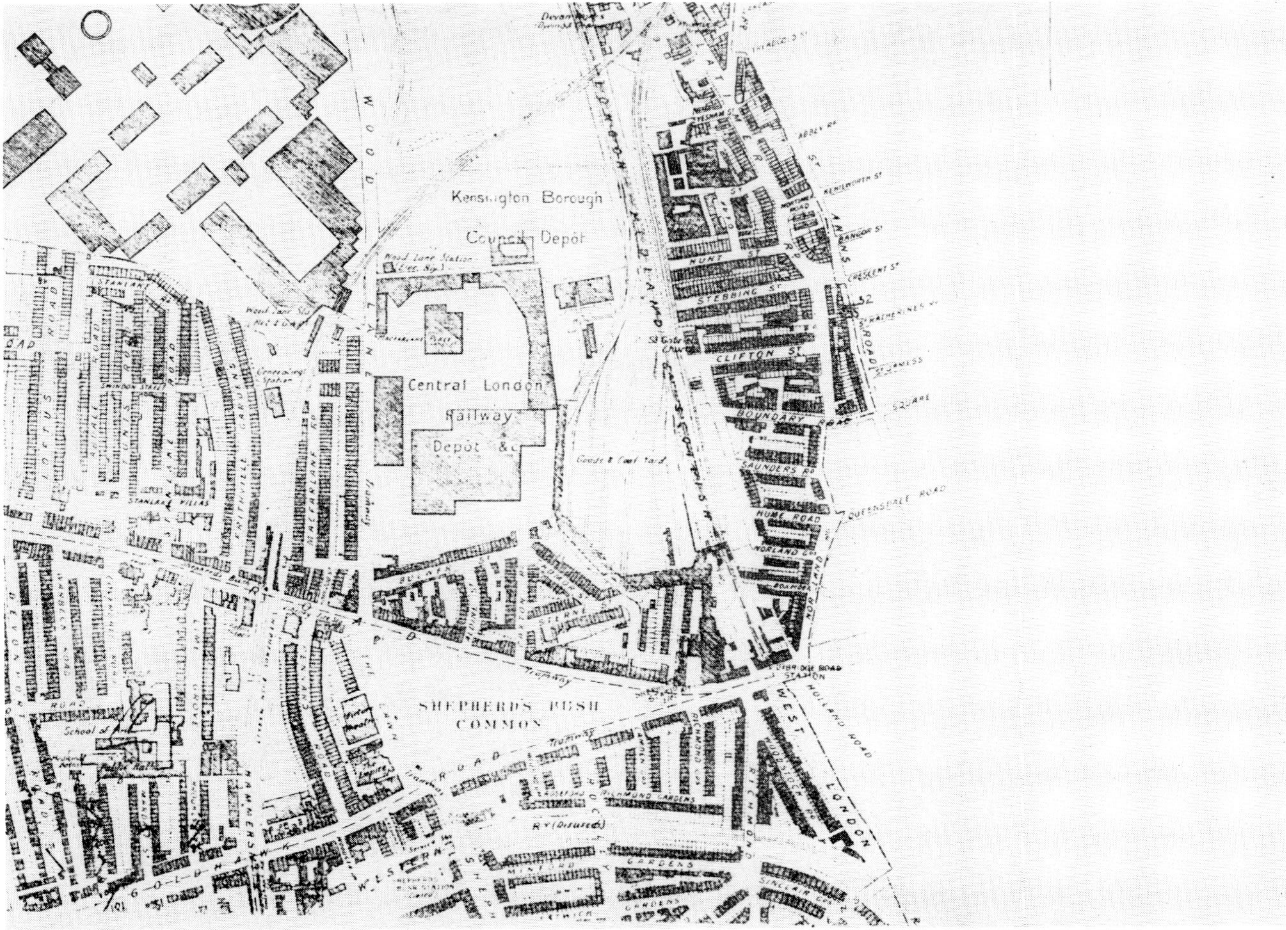

Ordnance Survey 1930

THE GROWTH AND DEVELOPMENT OF SHEPHERDS BUSH

Up until the end of the 18th century Shepherds Bush was just another piece of countryside around London, there was not even a village here, the nearest village being Hammersmith. Shepherds Bush lay astride one of the main routes into London from the west and the Green was a triangular piece of common land along the south side of the road.

When the rapid expansion of London took place in the 19th century it was well placed as an area of speculative building. It was not too far from the centre and was on a main routeway. During this century thousands of houses were built covering every available piece of land and the Green became a focus and service centre for the surrounding housing areas. By the beginning of the 20th century the appearance of the area was much the same as it was in the early 1960's.

The first half of this century was a period of relatively little change, but the second half has seen a lot of changes around the Green especially along the south side. Here the old shops have been replaced by a shopping precinct with a car park above. Beside this the old houses have been demolished and replaced by tower blocks and a large service station. Few of the original houses remain here and these have been recently under threat. The Uxbridge Road to the east of the Green has been made into an enormous roundabout to accommodate the link road to the A40(M) now the main through-road into the city.

The cinemas along the west side have now closed and their fate remains uncertain but office development seems the most likely option for any available areas around the Green. There has been a gradual run-down in the importance of the Green as a local service centre and there does not seem to be any signs of an upturn in its fortunes so far although anything is possible. How different will Shepherds Bush Green be by the year 2000?

The Lawns

The Lawns, bomb damage July 1944

CHURCHES

In the 19th century few Britons would have denied being Christians and most had a very genuine faith in their religion. The churches in addition to being places for prayer and worship, provided centres for much of the social life of their members. They appreciated the music and the sermons, and enthusiastically took part in group activities, helping the poor and invalids of the parishes and organising such things as choir and sunday-school outings in the summer. Not only did church members give generously to support their own church and clergy but they sent vast sums overseas, establishing schools and hospitals in India and Africa and mission fields all over the British Empire.

But West London too needed a mission. Here the population explosion was partly due to the fall in the mortality-rate but largely due to immigration from the home counties, which both caused and was in response to building development in the area. In 1868 the Bishop of London sent the Reverend William Handcock to evangelise the district. He had been trained by the Church Missionary Society and served them in India before coming to Shepherds Bush. Here he first preached in the streets in the open air, but quickly built schools and a substantial galvanised iron church with gothic windows in Richmond Road (now Richmond Way). This was the first Mission Church of St Simon, and was opened on Saturday, 30th December 1876. At about the same time the site in Rockley Road was purchased, and the foundation stone for a permanent church there was laid on 6th March 1879. His brother, Robert, was the first vicar of St Simon's.

A little earlier, in 1866, the Reverend E.J. May, of Nottingham, had applied for permission to build a church to be named after John the Baptist on the north west side of Holland Road. His application was rejected, but shortly afterwards a temporary iron structure was built for £1,700 by the Reverend George Booker on a site opposite, which had been made available by the failure of a builder. It was opened for divine service on 27th February 1869 with the Rev. Booker as incumbent and vicar designate. Apparently he had an evangelical manner of preaching, but the singing gave the impression of a high church. It could seat 900; half the places were free, but the other half were rented at prices from one guinea to thirty shillings a year. The offertory of about £330 was used for church expenses and to maintain the clergy. A school was connected with the church in which the choir-boys were educated free. On Sunday evenings the headmaster of Notting Hill Collegiate School gave lectures to appreciative congregations.

The site itself was purchased in 1875 for £1,100 after plans for a permanent church had been drawn up. It was built without the help of the Church Building Fund, and finished (apart from the west end) in 1892. After Booker's death some eighteen years later it was completed for a total cost of £25,000.

On 27th March 1880 a small band of Baptists, having failed to purchase the United Baptist and Congregational Norland Chapel when it was sold (eventually to be taken by the Salvation Army as Norland Castle), met at 6, Richmond Gardens and invited the Rev. George Pope to become their pastor and preach to them in Addison Hall. No definite stipend was offered to him; he was to receive whatever was given. He had a clear evangelical style, which was to attract large numbers of worshippers. In less than twelve months the congregation had so increased that Addison Hall was not big enough. A site at the top of Shepherds Bush Road was purchased for £750 freehold and a deposit of £150 paid. Within a few days a tent was erected and gospel services conducted there.

The First Tin Tabernacle (seating 200) was bought for £230 and opened on 4th December 1890, followed on 9th/10th December by the first sale of work which raised £85. A second iron building (seating about 600) was purchased for £140, but it did not comply with London County Council regulations. So, at a further cost of £1,600, permanent foundations were laid and walls 11 ft high were built, on which was placed the roof of the new iron building. This was called the Second Tin Tabernacle, and the small iron building at the back was used as a Sunday school. It too soon became very overcrowded as the church flourished. On 9th March 1907 memorial stones were laid, and the building of the permanent chapel progressed so rapidly that the opening ceremony was performed on 23rd June 1907. Less than two months later the pastor died. In only seventeen years he had seen his congregation increase from nineteen (including himself and his wife) meeting in a small hall to hundreds attending his services in a fine church.

During the tragic slaughter of the First World War. families of men at the front turned to the churches for prayer and consolation; church attendances increased markedly. Then, gradually, came disillusionment. Science seemed to offer truth: communism offered ideals. It became less fashionable to admit to being a Christian.

The Hammersmith Palais and theatres and cinemas offered agreeable alternatives to choir-practice and tough-provoking sermons. By the time of the Second World War there were more churches than were needed by the sizes of the congregations. And after it the numbers fell even more. The welfare state started to take over what previously had been the concern of parish clergy and church workers.

Then, however, came a new wave of immigrants (some prompted by the needs of the new national health service for doctors and nurses). This time they came from the British Commonwealth countries overseas - the very places that had been evangelised by our foreign missions a century before. Some brought their own religions, but many were staunch Christians, and as both clergy and just members of the congregations they brought a new vigour to our churches.

They bring much needed funds too. So perhaps we may look forward, for example, to the clock of St Simon's eventually being repaired to show that that church at least can keep up with the times.

BREWERIES AND PUBS

One hundred years ago there were two breweries to be found in Shepherds Bush. Of these the first established was the White Horse Brewery. The brewery was located at the corner of Shepherds Bush Green and Goldhawk Road, or New Road as it was then known. This site is now occupied by the Bush Hotel. The White Horse - not to be confused with the pub of the same name on the corner of Lime Grove and Uxbridge Road - was one of the oldest pubs in the area, dating back to before 1800. Beer continued to be brewed until 1899. At that date the premises were extensively rebuilt and the name changed to the Bush Hotel. An advert of 1876 not only extolled the brewery's beverages but also boasted the 'largest and best Quoit Ground in London'. Quoits was a game whereby a heavy flat ring was to be thrown as near as possible to a hob or pin.

The other brewery in Shepherds Bush one hundred years ago, the Albion Brewery, was on the south side of Uxbridge Road, near to the railway viaduct on a site now occupied by the Uxbridge Road Mini Market. The buildings were a brewery per se; unlike the White Horse, the Albion Brewery did not also serve as a pub. The Albion Brewery concern had originally been located in High Street, Kensington. However, at about 1870 the business was expanded by the then owners Messrs Richards with the acquisition of the site in Uxbridge Road. Brewing in Shepherds Bush continued for only forty years. In 1914 the brewery was demolished and the Silver Cinematograph Theatre constructed in its place. The Silver Cinema was itself destroyed by enemy action in the Second World War.

Along with the White Horse (now the Bush Hotel) the oldest pubs in Shepherds Bush are the Wellington Inn and the Beaumont Arms, both situated on the Uxbridge Road on the north side of the Green. All three pubs are listed in the Victuallers Recognizances or licencing returns for 1828-9. However, like the White Horse, both the Beaumont Arms and the Wellington were rebuilt in the early years of this century when the north side of Shepherds Bush Green was redeveloped.

Shepherds Bush Green seen from the railway bridge in Goldhawk Road, showing the Brewery Tavern c. 1876

The Royal Hotel, Norland Road c. 1900

The other three pubs in the immediate vicinity of Shepherds Bush Green, namely the Mail Coach, and the Telegraph, on opposite sides of the road at the Notting Hill end of the Green, and the Duke of Edinburgh on the corner of Richmond Way and Woodstock Grove, all date from the period between 1830 and 1880 when the population of Shepherds Bush expanded prodigiously with the coming of the railways and the growth of the suburbs.

The Mail Coach was completely rebuilt in the 1930's after it had been acquired by Goodhews Ltd. The pub, selling Watney's Ales, continues to be managed by Goodhews. Goodhews also managed two other local pubs, the Princess Victoria in Uxbridge Road and the Wellington.

The Telegraph was badly damaged by a bomb during the Second World War with more than thirty people killed and many injured. It was rebuilt as part of the development on the south side of Shepherds Bush Green which involved the building of the Shopping Precinct.

The one Shepherds Bush pub which has disappeared in recent times is the Royal which stood at the south end of Norland Road. This pub, which was a noted local landmark, was demolished as part of the road scheme involving the building of the roundabout in conjunction with the construction of the West Cross route from Westway.

ENTERTAINMENT ON THE GREEN
or

'A bird in the hand is worth two in Shepherds Bush!

Maisie Gay

Shepherds Bush Empire

Entertainment in Shepherds Bush began in earnest when the Shepherds Bush Empire, 'the Coliseum of West London', opened on the west side of the Green on 17th August 1903 and 'altered the neighbourhood from torpidity to vivacity and progress'.

Built at a cost of £50,000 to seat about 2,000 people, the architect was Frank Matcham, designer of the London Hippodrome. There was a Gala Performance on the opening night and the Karno Troup entertained (so records the Acton Gazette and Express), 'with cushioned seats in the gallery at threepence, velvet at fourpence and seats in the pit at sixpence', or one could really push the boat out and have a private box for four persons at 7/6 or 5/-.

The Acton Gazette lists Dan Leno, Marie Lloyd, George Robey, Vesta Tilley and Harry Lauder among the forthcoming attractions of the twice nightly variety performances. Steptoe senior remembers sitting on Marie Lloyd's knee at the Empire! George Robey, 'the best cure for pessimism', was certainly a favourite entertainer with his 'latest tarradiddles', as was Miss Vesta Tilley 'the idol of two hemispheres ... Her studies of masculine types are wonderfully true to life. She puts more real character into a turn of the arm, a tilt of the cigar, a step of the foot, than the majority of artistes put into a whole song'. (Raved the West London Observer in May 1916.)

'Miss Gertie Gitana: the star who never fails to shine' - is a typical advertisement of that time. George Formby was another star who shone in 1916. 'He will appear in his latest successes and probably "warble" the song he sang before the King and Queen at the Royal Performance last year, "We all went to Leicester Square", among others'. 'I've had my voice insured for £20,000', said Mr Formby, 'and I'm in full benefit'.

The Empire in its day presented such an immensity of talent that names flood to mind that are too numerous to list. A great favourite of music hall audiences were cross-talk comedians and none more so than the duo acts of Naughton & Gold, Nervo & Knox, and Flanagan & Allen who all performed here. These "turns" later combined to form the internationally famous Victoria Palace Crazy Gang. The later addition to this loony lot, Monsewer Eddie Gray, was also a favourite at Shepherds Bush.

It is unlikely that any who saw the act which the Empire advertised as "Ted & Barbara Andrews and

The Shepherds Bush Empire, The Palladium
and the Pavilion c. 1923

STATE OFFICE
THE LAWN SHEPHERDS BUSH

daughter Julie" could visualise that "daughter Julie" would someday be the Julie Andrews of international fame. Many Shepherds Bush residents will have fond memories of Ethel Revnell & Gracie West, Elsie & Doris Waters, Donald Peers and the Wilson, Keppel & Betty sand dance act. The list could continue almost ad infinitum with Max Wall, Max Miller, Jimmy Jewel & Ben Warris, etc.

Mention must be made of the times when the strains of "Somebody's stole my girl" were sufficient to indicate that the Billy Cotton Band Show was on stage. Another instrumental group much favoured was the Nat Gonella Band as also the so-called musical rendition provided by Sid Milward & his Nitwits.

The Shepherds Bush Empire continued successfully for many years, though the character of the entertainment changed as the days of variety passed away to be replaced by revue. There began to be competition, chiefly from the picture houses, but also of a less significant though perhaps more irritating nature. 'Regarding the bandstand', complained the Manager of the Empire to the Town Clerk, Hammersmith Borough Council in 1946, 'might I ask the favour that it be moved further on the Green ... the music from the brass bands could be heard inside the Theatre, and was rather disturbing in a quiet part of the play in action'.

In 1953, fifty years after its much lauded opening night, the Shepherds Bush Empire was taken over by the BBC as a television theatre. 'Last Saturday night saw the last night of Shepherds Bush Empire as a music hall', wrote the Performer on 1st October 1953, 'in future it will be just one more studio for the BBC to stage television programmes before invited, yet restricted audiences ... Saturday night's audience paid tribute ... in their enthusiasm, and at the end, when the company, members of the staff and the patrons joined in singing "Auld Lang Syne" and then the National Anthem ... The company at the Bush for its final week included Hal Monty, Robb Wilton, Krysta & Krystal, Stan Stennett, Dawn White and her Glamazons, Allen Bros. and June, Tow Condons and Tessa Smallpage'.

The Empire remains a BBC theatre, but it still has its moments. 'A radiant Princess Margaret steps out of the Television Theatre at Shepherds Bush Green after watching a live broadcast of "What's My Line?" ' noted a local newspaper on 28th December 1956. 'She broke a strict rule by moving about the studio during actual transmission, but T.V. chiefs willingly gave permission. The Princess also achieved fame by singing "You can't chop your mamma up in Massachusetts" in the control room'.

Bush Theatre

The theatrical tradition of the Empire was revived twenty years later on the Green by the opening on 6th April 1972 of the Bush Theatre in an adapted hall above the Bush Hotel (home of many Irish pub songs). Called the Alternative Theatre Company, the three directors, John Neville, Brian McDermott (who started the pub theatre at King's Head, Islington), and Andrew Barton, 'aimed to create the sort of theatre that would appeal to the ordinary man in the street - less formal, less expensive and nearer home'.

Opening with John Fowles' The Collector (the entire QPR team apparently attended the first night), this theatre has seen many successful productions, the policy always being 'to put on new plays by little known writers using established actors'. John McGrath's Plugged In had its first performance here. The work of playwrights such as Snoo Wilson and David Edgar have been given exposure, and of Stephen Poliakoff, whose Hitting Town and City Sugar went on to be successes. John Arden's much praised The Ballygombeen Bequest was staged at the Bush as was Tom Kempinski's Duet for One with Frances de la Tour.

Seating around a hundred people on wooden blocks around a moveable open stage, conditions at the Bush are rather cramped (only one dressing room for all the actors), but it is a popular theatre with good actors and is still going strong.

Palladium Cinema

The Palladium Cinema opened next door to the Empire in about 1910 as the Cinematograph Theatre, it may also have been known in the early days as Pyke's Playhouse. A resident of Shepherds Bush recalled in 1962 'I remember when some fifty years ago or more, one of the first cinemas opened in Shepherds Bush, London, the Management charged only threepence a seat - and cups of tea and biscuits were passed round in the afternoon. How times change!'

The Cinematograph was renamed the Palladium Cinema in about 1916-24; it subsequently became the Essoldo in 1955, the Classic in 1972 and Odeon 2 in 1973. In October 1981 Rank closed it down, along with a number of other Odeon cinemas in London, and it remains out of use.

Silver Cinema

The Silver Cinema, 11 Uxbridge Road, opened in about 1914 and operated until September 1940 when it was closed as a result of bomb damage. The site is now part of the Shepherds Bush Market extension.

The cinema was showing Eddie Cantor in Forty Little Mothers and Jack Buchanan in Bulldog sees it Through at the time it was hit.

Pavilion Cinema

The Pavilion Cinema opened next to the Palladium on 16th August 1923, with a capacity of 3,000. Designed by architect Frank T. Verity, it rather surprisingly won the RIBA London Street Architecture Award for 'the best frontage completed during the year 1923 within the radius of four miles of Charing Cross'. Sir Edward Lutyens was one of the judges, as was Mr (later Sir) Guy Dawber who, according to Dennis Sharp in his The Picture Palace, 'found the Pavilion an imposing structure of brick and stone in which the former material especially is used with great imagination'. 'It was indeed a great step forward in English cinema design', continues Mr Shapr, 'although the interior was little more than an emasculated version of a typical music hall'.

Verity took the great Roman baths as his theme, the chief of which was built in about AD 208 and named after the Emperor Caracalla, whose bust was to be found in the foyer of the cinema. While 'Roman' red brick was used outside, the interior colour scheme was a blending of three shades of copper.

The cinema was badly damaged by a doodlebug in July 1944 and remained closed for eleven years, when it was eventually repaired, modernised and reopened as the Gaumont in July 1955, with a reduced seating capacity (about 2,000). Renamed the Odeon Cinema in 1962, it was remodelled again in 1970 as a Top Rank Club for bingo and films, but sadly by 1984 the bingo has taken over completely and the old Pavilion Cinema is no more.

TRANSPORT

Shepherds Bush lies on the main road from London to Oxford, Cheltenham, Gloucester, Hereford, South Wales and the South Midlands.

By the 15th century coach travel was commonplace. In 1669 Shepherds Bush was on the route of a London-Oxford service (the journey taking a day), and by the early 18th century coaches to all the above mentioned places were passing through Shepherds Bush. These services were to improve and expand to reach their zenith in the early years of the 19th century.

The opening of the Liverpool & Manchester railway in 1830 was to sound the doom of horse-drawn stage coaches, the system disappearing in only eight years though the last mail coach survived till 1875. It was to be about one hundred years before road travel was to return as a viable form of transport of which more later.

Shepherds Bush Green 1920

Shepherds Bush Green c. 1930

Railways and Underground

The railway came to Shepherds Bush on 27th May 1844 only to close on 1st December of that year and it remained closed till 1st November 1869. Originally called Shepherds Bush it was reopened with the less precise title Uxbridge Road. The station finally closed (after wartime bombing of the line) on 21st October 1940.

The opening of the Hammersmith & City Railway on 13th June 1864 provided the area with a truly local service. Shepherds Bush station opened on the same day and was situated half-way along the market. This station was replaced by two new stations called Goldhawk Road and Shepherds Bush on the 1st April 1914. Tramway competition had taken its toll of traffic from this inconveniently sited station. The line was electrified on 5th November 1906. A station named Wood Lane was opened on 1st May 1908, re-named White City on 28th November 1947 and closed due to fire damage on 25th October 1959.

On 1st May 1874 a third Shepherds Bush station was opened in Shepherds Bush Road on a site opposite the Grampians. This station was on the L. & SWR line from Kensington to Richmond via Shepherds Bush and Hammersmith. It was closed on 5th June 1916 as a war-time economy measure and never reopened. As a "what might have been" there was a proposal for an extension of the Central London Railway to Richmond using that station and track.

The Central London Railway was the last of the rail-ways and was opened on 30th July 1900 with yet another station named Shepherds Bush. This line was nick-named "the twopenny tube" and ran from Bank to Shepherds Bush. It was the first line to have a uniform fare system of twopence a journey. An extension opened on 14th May 1908 at Wood Lane; this station was replaced by the present White City station on 23rd November 1947.

Tramways and Trolleybuses

The first tramway was opened between Uxbridge Road station and the Queen Victoria pub on 1st June 1874, and closed on 20th February 1875. It reopened on 21st September the same year and extended to Acton High Street on 18th February 1878. A tramway line along Goldhawk Road to Youngs Corner opened on 18th November 1882. The London United Tramways took over these services and started electrifying them, the first one was electrified on 10th July 1901. The London County Council started an electric tram service on 30th May 1908 from Hammersmith via Shepherds Bush to Harlesden.

The trams were replaced by trolleybuses in the 1930's as follows:

The Goldhawk Rd service 27th Oct. 1935
The Uxbridge Rd service 15th Nov. 1936
The Shepherds Bush Rd/Wood Lane service 12th Sept. 1937

The trolleybus services were themselves replaced by buses in reverse order as follows:

Shepherds Bush/Wood Lane	19th July 1960
Uxbridge Road	8th Nov. 1960
Goldhawk Road	8th May 1962

The Goldhawk Road line was the last one of the trolleybus operations in London and saw the closure of the largest system in the world.

Buses and Coaches

It is notoriously difficult to give an accurate history of bus services. Unlike trams, trolleybuses and railways there is little or nothing to indicate that a service was operated. Take away the bus stops and who would know what buses operated on any street.

While coach travel declined local bus services (horse-drawn) started to flourish and by 1850 some 1,300 vehicles were licenced. Services were provided along the Uxbridge Road to Ealing and Southall. Horse-bus services expanded during the latter half of the 19th century with the London General Omnibus Company playing a major role.

Shepherds Bush Green on a foggy morning

RAILWAY LINES AND STATIONS IN FULHAM AND HAMMERSMITH

NOTES
1. Some details have been simplified
2. The section of the Great Western Railway from Wood Lane to Ealing Broadway via East Acton is now part of the Central Line

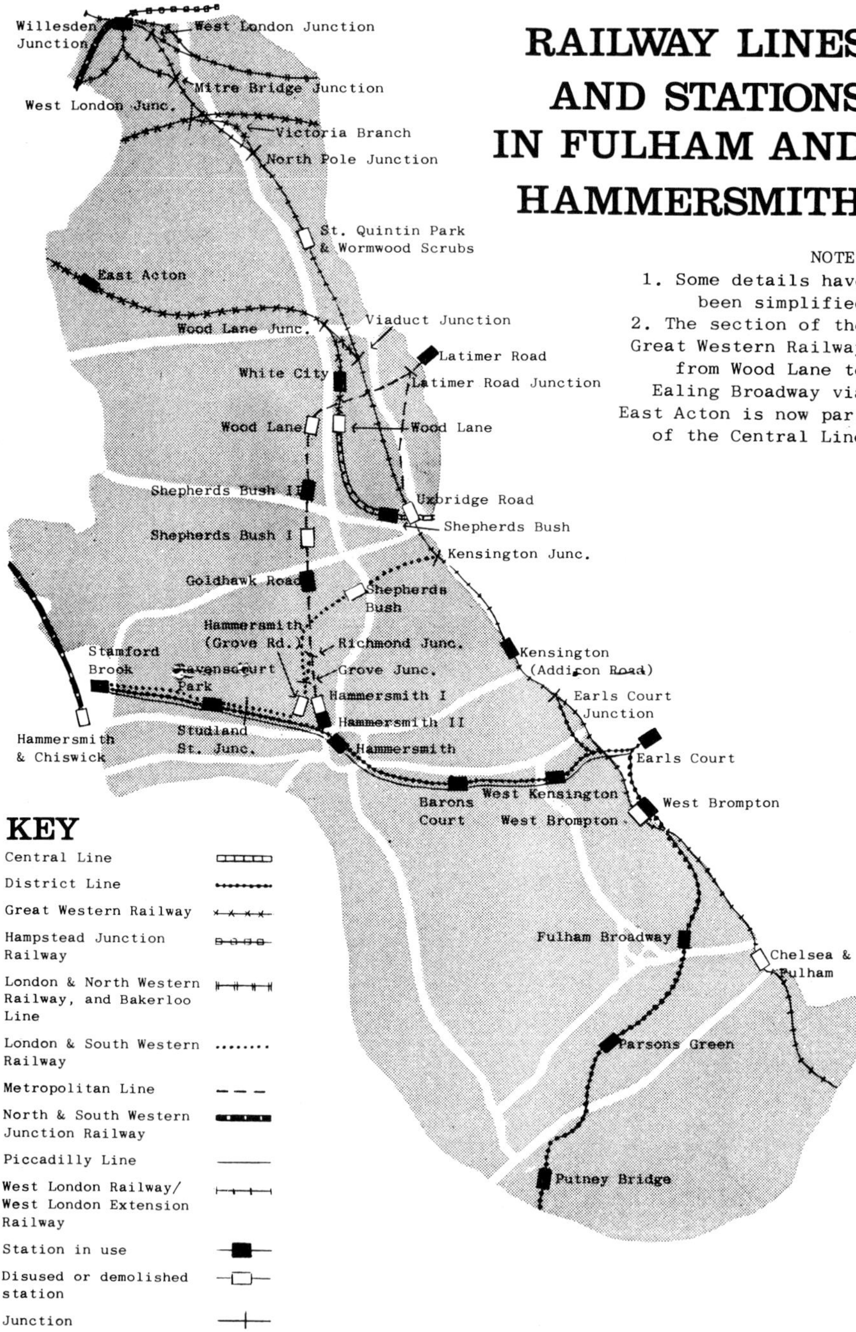

The early 1900's saw the development of the petrol engine bus. The LGOC produced its successful B.type and the days of the horse-drawn bus were doomed, the need for horses in the First World War finally killing off any remaining services.

The First World War caused a severe contraction of bus services. Shepherds Bush being well served by trams and railways did not suffer unduly by the cuts in services. The end of the war in 1918 started a process of expansion of services to their former level and beyond. The needs of war had caused improvements in design and the post war buses were great improvements. It is worth noting that during the Second World War history repeated itself but Shepherds Bush was again well served by its new trolleybuses and trains.

As a result of the bus development excursion traffic was developed and the success of this was to produce a return of the coach in stage service, the horse being replaced by a petrol engine. Green Line coaches started services in July 1930 and the services expanded. the threat of the Second World War caused services to be withdrawn on 31st August 1939. Limited services were restored on 17th January 1940 but the blitz and torpedoing of tankers caused the final withdrawal on 29th September 1942.

Green Line services were restored on 6th February 1946 and soon virtually all services were running except along the Goldhawk Road. It is worth noting that all roads from Shepherds Bush Green had a service at some time or other, Holland Park Avenue during the 1930's and Wood Lane in 1964/5. The coming of mass car ownership saw a general contraction of all public services and Green Line now operate along Shepherds Bush Road only.

Bus and underground services have been cut in recent years but still in general give good services with 10 bus routes serving the Green.

Recent changes in transport policy have seen this trend reversed and a feasibility study is under way on the reopening of the line between Clapham Junction and Willesden Junction for passenger traffic.

WHITE CITY & THE GREAT EXHIBITION

In 1905, based on an idea of the French Chamber of Commerce and endorsed by King Edward VII, two architects - one British, Imre Kiralfy, and one French, Marius Toudoire - were commissioned to design and build an exhibition complex on an area of common land at Shepherds Bush to the west of Wood Lane and south of Wormwood Scrubs.

Kiralfy and Toudoire created fantastical gardens, covering over 200 acres which was one of the most architectually ambitious projects ever undertaken. Kiralfy employed 4,000 workers by day and 2,000 workers by night who worked by the light of huge electric floodlights, to complete the immense task of constructing all the twenty palaces and 120 exhibition halls, including eight halls which measured 400 ft long and 70 ft wide and stood on steel pillars 30 ft above ground level. Within the grounds of this pleasure-land, Kiralfy built half-a-mile of canals and waterways including a magic lagoon known as the 'Court of Honour'. The buildings were intricately embellished in 'neo-rococco ornamentation' and outlined in electric lights; the semi-circular cascade at the head of the lagoon shone with many colours as the water cascaded over a series of multi-coloured glass steps.

A guide book to Hammersmith at that time mentions the White City as 'something like a revolution was effected in this particular corner of Greater London with the opening of this wonderful city of white dwellings, which, with its far-famed Court of Honour and its countless thousands of electric lights, proved one of the most charming spectacles of which England could boast'.

The White City, so called because of its intricate white buildings and waterways resembling Venice, was built to house the Franco-British Exhibition of 1908, and this exhibition was designed to strengthen Anglo-French ties. The exhibition itself was opened by the Prince and Princess of Wales, in the rain, on 14th May. The exhibition was such a success that 120,000 people visited it on the first day. With the exhibition site in mind, two new stations were built, one

Court **of** Honour, Franco-British Exhibition
White City 1908.

General view of the White City, 1908

on the Hammersmith and City line (Wood Lane) and one on the twopenny tube - now the Central Line - (White City), to cope with the expected large number of visitors. Indeed, when the exhibition closed on 31st October 1908 $8\frac{1}{2}$ million people had visited it, including many national and international dignitories and royalty. King Edward VII visited the exhibition with the President of France, Monsieur Fallieres shortly after the opening, and Queen Alexandra and Princess Victoria also visited it.

After the Franco-British Exhibition a series of international exhibitions were held at the White City, including the highly acclaimed and very successful Japan-British Exhibition of 1910. The annual exhibitions were stopped when the Great War broke out in 1914 and the grounds were then used for military training and the halls for war work, i.e. making tents, aeroplanes, etc., and a recruiting centre was set up at the Uxbridge Road entrance.

After the war the White City failed to get back into its pre-war stride and it was decided not to continue the series of annual exhibitions which had become such a feature of Shepherds Bush life. Apart from a few small exhibitions, including the London section of the British Industries Fair in 1921 and the Cotton Fair in the early 1930's, the area was not used and became derelict. It was then cleared and the present White City estate built, the only remains of the great exhibition area are Hammersmith Park and the names of the roads on the estate.

White City Stadium

The stadium was built at the same time as the exhibition area and the 1908 Olympic Games were staged here with Dorando Pietri's dramatic finish in the marathon and his subsequent disqualification due to some 'well-meaning' officials helping him to his feet in the last hundred yards of the race, but he was later awarded a special gold cup by Queen Alexandra.

When it was built the White City stadium was the largest of its kind in the world. It housed 150,000 spectators when filled to capacity. The stadium is now the only remaining functional part of the White

City Exhibition. The stadium has remained in virtual constant use since the Olympic Games in 1908. On 27th June 1927 the first ever greyhound meeting in Britain was held here and since 1932 the 3 'A's athletics championships have also been held here.

THE WHITE CITY - TAILPIECE

The many years that have rolled since the Great Exhibition first opened its doors have made it impossible to find a witness to its earliest splendours. There are, however, quite a few whose age permits them interesting recollections of the time around the First World War period which was not that long after the exhibitions prime. One such account is given below by a Shepherds Bush resident of over sixty years standing:

"As a four-year-old the first thing I learnt about the White City was that it was the place where my aunt worked. I was told she was on war work and as a child found it confusing that my father also on war work did not work with her. Subsequently it turned out that my father, medically unfit for military service, was doing his stint on war weapons with Wilkinson Sword Co. of Acton. So what was my aunt doing at White City? I soon discovered that her job there was heavy machine-sewing work. This mainly comprised the stitching of tough white canvas to make tents, kit-bags, nosebags for horses and similar appurtenances of war. Another thing, in those days, well before the plastics age, war restrictions on metals meant that buckets were in short supply and waterproof canvas was used as a make-shift. Many of the substitute sewn canvas buckets supplied for military use had their origins in the old exhibition area and this was only a small portion of the emergency industries set up in the old halls.

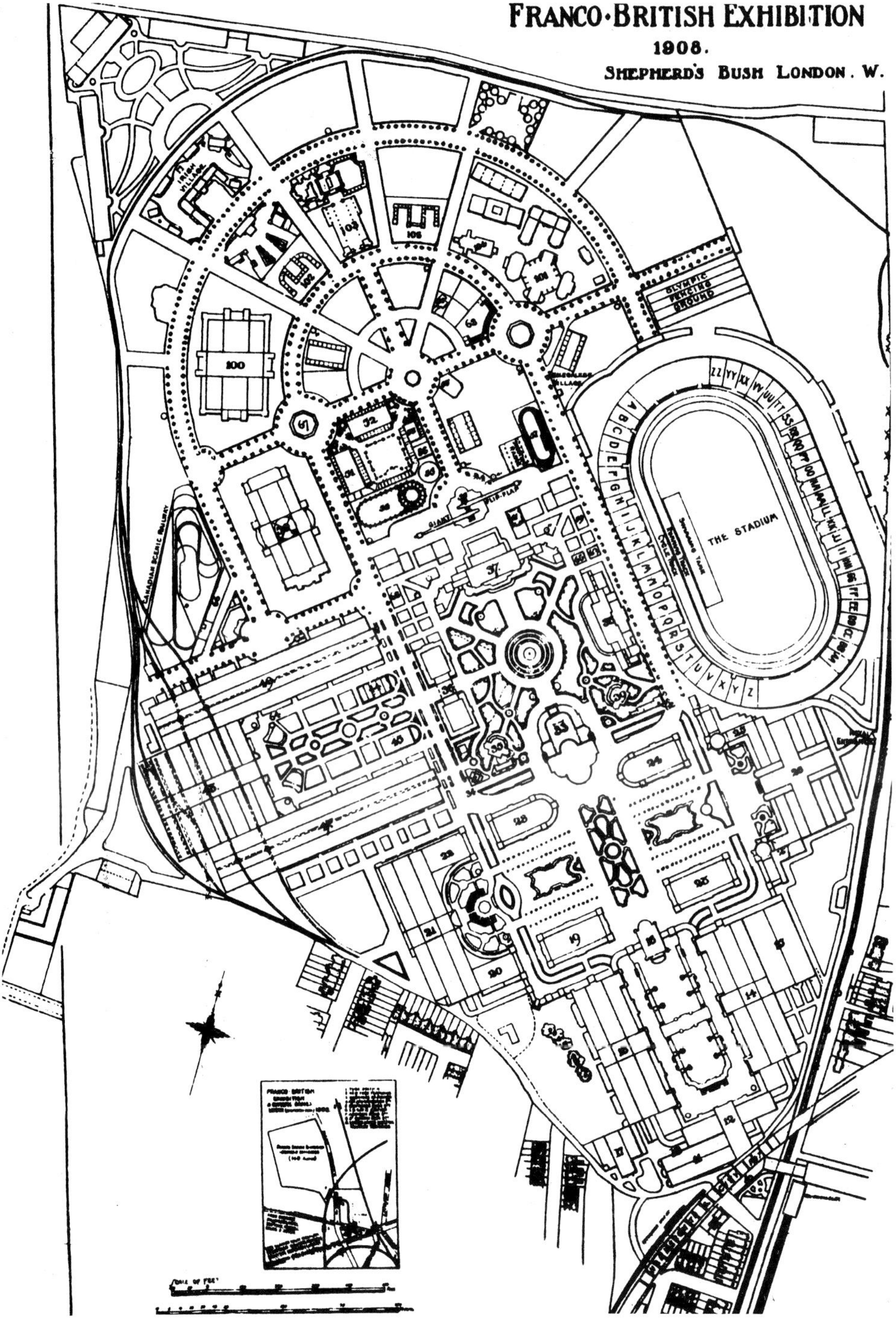
FRANCO·BRITISH EXHIBITION
1908.
SHEPHERD'S BUSH LONDON. W.
IRISH VILLAGE
OLYMPIC FENCING GROUND
THE STADIUM
CANADIAN SCENIC RAILWAY
100
105
37
19
20
14

Norland Road c. 1900

By about 1920 I had become familiar with both Shepherds Bush and Wood Lane entrances and I must say that they looked very much then as they appeared in the pictures of their early days. Allow of course the greyish tinge which London's atmosphere had deposited, remove the decorative flags and still to be seen were the ornate stucco mouldings which were the exhibition's distinguishing features. Other external evidence was the presence of the still standing boundary walls, the one on the eastern side consisting of about half-a-mile of unbroken high wooden fencing stretching northwards from Wood Lane entrance along Wood Lane till it stopped at the railings bordering the Central London Railway (Central Line). This fence seemed to be a tough kind of match-boarding, tongued and grooved (you couldn't peep between its planks), about 10 ft high, painted white and the top of each of its planks cut into a distinctive circular pattern. Having spoken of an unbroken half-a-mile of fencing I need to explain that Westway had yet to be built, that at strategic points fence sections were hinged to make gates for vehicle access and similarly for entrance to the stadium.

An identical style of fencing and entrance ways was also used for the western boundary, the southernmost point of which commenced immediately behind St Stephen's Parish Hall which was then situated at the corner of Ellerslie and Bloemfontein Roads. It ran northwards along the course of Bloemfontein Road and ended up by butting into the right-hand parapet of the footbridge at the front of Hammersmith Hospital. Since the northern boundary was not accessible by reason of the railway and the southern obscured by the QPR football ground and the backs of houses, the style of these boundaries cannot be confirmed. It could reliably be presumed that the same style of barrier had been erected north and south as two sections of it could be seen cutting off the endings of both Loftus Road and Frithville Gardens.

I have used the present name, Hammersmith Hospital for the building then known as the Workhouse and Dispensary although at the time I have in mind it was caring for the war wounded and a few of the older residents of Shepherds Bush may well remember them in pale blue uniforms taking the air on the verandahs facing Du Cane Road.

I am not much good at dates but it must have been in the early 1920's that a minor exhibition was staged in one or two of the halls still in good preservation. I remember it for four reasons: One - it was the first time I had managed to get inside the boundary walls (entry by the Wood Lane gate entrance). Two - I got a free box of caramels on admission. Three - I saw a typewriter in operation for the first time. Four - I was intrigued by the mechanics of an automatic printing machine which was, before my very eyes, producing copies of Millais' picture "Bubbles" on behalf of Pears Soap.

About some ten years later I noticed that the towers, either side of the Shepherds Bush entrance, were being restored and discovered that a British Industries Fair was to be held there. Unlike later, the public were able to gain admittance andI remember it only for the razor I bought there. Up to then all safety razors had comb-like prongs (early Gillette type). To the best of my knowledge, I was able to buy at this exhibition, the first of the now commonplace combless type. That is about all I can remember before present developments took over.'

The term 'present developments' conjures up such a host of applications and usages to which White City is tied that excuses are sought for only mentioning the following: To some it is a housing estate, others think of it only as an underground station, the one you want if the stadium has an athletic programme, the dog track is in use or QPR again do well enough to use it for a season. A few years back the roar of Speedway could be heard and a military tattoo is by no means unknown. Throughout the world however, the magic name 'White City' means the headquarters of BBC Television, as it does to those invited to watch some of its transmissions. It seems that the genius of Imre Kiralfy in decorating 200 acres of Shepherds Bush scrubland with brilliant white buildings promoted a name which will endure for ever.

Laying a drain through the site of Shepherds Bush Market, 1906.

"Nothing changes" - Shepherds Bush Green 1910